NAME

M000107554

GIFT IDEAS

BUDGET   ACTUAL

STORE/GIFT

☐ ORDERED?   ☐ WRAPPED? ☐ SENT/GIVEN?

NOTES

NAME

GIFT IDEAS

BUDGET   ACTUAL

STORE/GIFT

☐ ORDERED?   ☐ WRAPPED? ☐ SENT/GIVEN?

NOTES

NAME

GIFT IDEAS

BUDGET   ACTUAL

STORE/GIFT

☐ ORDERED?   ☐ WRAPPED? ☐ SENT/GIVEN?

NOTES

NAME

GIFT IDEAS

BUDGET   ACTUAL

STORE/GIFT

☐ ORDERED?   ☐ WRAPPED? ☐ SENT/GIVEN?

NOTES

NAME

GIFT IDEAS

BUDGET   ACTUAL

STORE/GIFT

☐ ORDERED?   ☐ WRAPPED? ☐ SENT/GIVEN?

NOTES

NAME

GIFT IDEAS

BUDGET   ACTUAL

STORE/GIFT

☐ ORDERED?   ☐ WRAPPED?   ☐ SENT/GIVEN?

NOTES

NAME

GIFT IDEAS

BUDGET   ACTUAL

STORE/GIFT

☐ ORDERED?   ☐ WRAPPED?   ☐ SENT/GIVEN?

NOTES

NAME

GIFT IDEAS

BUDGET   ACTUAL

STORE/GIFT

☐ ORDERED?   ☐ WRAPPED?   ☐ SENT/GIVEN?

NOTES

NAME

GIFT IDEAS

BUDGET   ACTUAL

STORE/GIFT

☐ ORDERED?   ☐ WRAPPED? ☐ SENT/GIVEN?

NOTES

NAME

GIFT IDEAS

BUDGET   ACTUAL

STORE/GIFT

☐ ORDERED?   ☐ WRAPPED? ☐ SENT/GIVEN?

NOTES

NAME

GIFT IDEAS

BUDGET   ACTUAL

STORE/GIFT

☐ ORDERED?   ☐ WRAPPED? ☐ SENT/GIVEN?

NOTES

NAME

GIFT IDEAS

BUDGET   ACTUAL

STORE/GIFT

☐ ORDERED?   ☐ WRAPPED? ☐ SENT/GIVEN?

NOTES

NAME

GIFT IDEAS

BUDGET   ACTUAL

STORE/GIFT

☐ ORDERED?   ☐ WRAPPED?   ☐ SENT/GIVEN?

NOTES

NAME

GIFT IDEAS

BUDGET   ACTUAL

STORE/GIFT

☐ ORDERED?   ☐ WRAPPED? ☐ SENT/GIVEN?

NOTES

NAME

GIFT IDEAS

BUDGET   ACTUAL

STORE/GIFT

☐ ORDERED?   ☐ WRAPPED? ☐ SENT/GIVEN?

NOTES

NAME

GIFT IDEAS

BUDGET ACTUAL

STORE/GIFT

☐ ORDERED?　☐ WRAPPED?　☐ SENT/GIVEN?

NOTES

NAME

GIFT IDEAS

BUDGET   ACTUAL

STORE/GIFT

☐ ORDERED?   ☐ WRAPPED? ☐ SENT/GIVEN?

NOTES

NAME

GIFT IDEAS

BUDGET   ACTUAL

STORE/GIFT

☐ ORDERED?   ☐ WRAPPED?   ☐ SENT/GIVEN?

NOTES

NAME

GIFT IDEAS

BUDGET   ACTUAL

STORE/GIFT

☐ ORDERED?   ☐ WRAPPED?   ☐ SENT/GIVEN?

NOTES

NAME

GIFT IDEAS

BUDGET   ACTUAL

STORE/GIFT

☐ ORDERED?   ☐ WRAPPED? ☐ SENT/GIVEN?

NOTES

NAME

GIFT IDEAS

BUDGET   ACTUAL

STORE/GIFT

☐ ORDERED?   ☐ WRAPPED?   ☐ SENT/GIVEN?

NOTES

NAME

GIFT IDEAS

BUDGET   ACTUAL

STORE/GIFT

☐ ORDERED?   ☐ WRAPPED?   ☐ SENT/GIVEN?

NOTES

NAME

GIFT IDEAS

BUDGET   ACTUAL

STORE/GIFT

☐ ORDERED?   ☐ WRAPPED? ☐ SENT/GIVEN?

NOTES

NAME

GIFT IDEAS

BUDGET   ACTUAL

STORE/GIFT

☐ ORDERED?   ☐ WRAPPED?   ☐ SENT/GIVEN?

NOTES

NAME

GIFT IDEAS

BUDGET   ACTUAL

STORE/GIFT

☐ ORDERED?   ☐ WRAPPED?   ☐ SENT/GIVEN?

NOTES

NAME

GIFT IDEAS

BUDGET   ACTUAL

STORE/GIFT

☐ ORDERED?   ☐ WRAPPED?   ☐ SENT/GIVEN?

NOTES

NAME

GIFT IDEAS

BUDGET   ACTUAL

STORE/GIFT

☐ ORDERED?   ☐ WRAPPED? ☐ SENT/GIVEN?

NOTES

NAME

GIFT IDEAS

BUDGET   ACTUAL

STORE/GIFT

☐ ORDERED?   ☐ WRAPPED?   ☐ SENT/GIVEN?

NOTES

NAME

GIFT IDEAS

BUDGET   ACTUAL

STORE/GIFT

☐ ORDERED?   ☐ WRAPPED? ☐ SENT/GIVEN?

NOTES

NAME

GIFT IDEAS

BUDGET   ACTUAL

STORE/GIFT

☐ ORDERED?   ☐ WRAPPED?   ☐ SENT/GIVEN?

NOTES

NAME

GIFT IDEAS

BUDGET   ACTUAL

STORE/GIFT

☐ ORDERED?   ☐ WRAPPED? ☐ SENT/GIVEN?

NOTES

NAME

GIFT IDEAS

BUDGET   ACTUAL

STORE/GIFT

☐ ORDERED?   ☐ WRAPPED? ☐ SENT/GIVEN?

NOTES

NAME

GIFT IDEAS

BUDGET   ACTUAL

STORE/GIFT

☐ ORDERED?   ☐ WRAPPED? ☐ SENT/GIVEN?

NOTES

NAME

GIFT IDEAS

BUDGET   ACTUAL

STORE/GIFT

☐ ORDERED?   ☐ WRAPPED?   ☐ SENT/GIVEN?

NOTES

NAME

GIFT IDEAS

BUDGET   ACTUAL

STORE/GIFT

☐ ORDERED?   ☐ WRAPPED? ☐ SENT/GIVEN?

NOTES

NAME

GIFT IDEAS

BUDGET   ACTUAL

STORE/GIFT

☐ ORDERED?   ☐ WRAPPED? ☐ SENT/GIVEN?

NOTES

NAME

GIFT IDEAS

BUDGET   ACTUAL

STORE/GIFT

☐ ORDERED?   ☐ WRAPPED? ☐ SENT/GIVEN?

NOTES

NAME

GIFT IDEAS

BUDGET   ACTUAL

STORE/GIFT

☐ ORDERED?   ☐ WRAPPED?   ☐ SENT/GIVEN?

NOTES

NAME

GIFT IDEAS

BUDGET	ACTUAL

STORE/GIFT

☐ ORDERED?   ☐ WRAPPED?   ☐ SENT/GIVEN?

NOTES

NAME

GIFT IDEAS

BUDGET   ACTUAL

STORE/GIFT

☐ ORDERED?   ☐ WRAPPED? ☐ SENT/GIVEN?

NOTES

NAME

GIFT IDEAS

BUDGET   **ACTUAL**

STORE/GIFT

☐ ORDERED?   ☐ WRAPPED? ☐ SENT/GIVEN?

NOTES

NAME

GIFT IDEAS

BUDGET   ACTUAL

STORE/GIFT

☐ ORDERED?   ☐ WRAPPED?   ☐ SENT/GIVEN?

NOTES

NAME

GIFT IDEAS

BUDGET   ACTUAL

STORE/GIFT

☐ ORDERED?   ☐ WRAPPED? ☐ SENT/GIVEN?

NOTES

NAME

GIFT IDEAS

BUDGET   ACTUAL

STORE/GIFT

☐ ORDERED?   ☐ WRAPPED?   ☐ SENT/GIVEN?

NOTES

NAME

GIFT IDEAS

BUDGET   ACTUAL

STORE/GIFT

□ ORDERED?   □ WRAPPED?   □ SENT/GIVEN?

NOTES

NAME

GIFT IDEAS

BUDGET   ACTUAL

STORE/GIFT

☐ ORDERED?   ☐ WRAPPED? ☐ SENT/GIVEN?

NOTES

NAME

GIFT IDEAS

BUDGET   ACTUAL

STORE/GIFT

☐ ORDERED?   ☐ WRAPPED? ☐ SENT/GIVEN?

NOTES

NAME

GIFT IDEAS

BUDGET   ACTUAL

STORE/GIFT

☐ ORDERED?   ☐ WRAPPED?   ☐ SENT/GIVEN?

NOTES

NAME

GIFT IDEAS

BUDGET   ACTUAL

STORE/GIFT

☐ ORDERED?   ☐ WRAPPED? ☐ SENT/GIVEN?

NOTES

NAME

GIFT IDEAS

BUDGET   ACTUAL

STORE/GIFT

☐ ORDERED?   ☐ WRAPPED?   ☐ SENT/GIVEN?

NOTES

NAME

GIFT IDEAS

BUDGET   ACTUAL

STORE/GIFT

☐ ORDERED?   ☐ WRAPPED? ☐ SENT/GIVEN?

NOTES

NAME

GIFT IDEAS

BUDGET   ACTUAL

STORE/GIFT

☐ ORDERED?   ☐ WRAPPED?   ☐ SENT/GIVEN?

NOTES

NAME

GIFT IDEAS

BUDGET   ACTUAL

STORE/GIFT

☐ ORDERED?   ☐ WRAPPED?   ☐ SENT/GIVEN?

NOTES

NAME

GIFT IDEAS

BUDGET   ACTUAL

STORE/GIFT

☐ ORDERED?   ☐ WRAPPED?   ☐ SENT/GIVEN?

NOTES

NAME

GIFT IDEAS

BUDGET   ACTUAL

STORE/GIFT

☐ ORDERED?   ☐ WRAPPED? ☐ SENT/GIVEN?

NOTES

NAME

GIFT IDEAS

BUDGET   ACTUAL

STORE/GIFT

☐ ORDERED?   ☐ WRAPPED?   ☐ SENT/GIVEN?

NOTES

NAME

GIFT IDEAS

BUDGET   ACTUAL

STORE/GIFT

☐ ORDERED?   ☐ WRAPPED?   ☐ SENT/GIVEN?

NOTES

NAME

GIFT IDEAS

BUDGET   ACTUAL

STORE/GIFT

☐ ORDERED?   ☐ WRAPPED? ☐ SENT/GIVEN?

NOTES

NAME

GIFT IDEAS

BUDGET   ACTUAL

STORE/GIFT

☐ ORDERED?   ☐ WRAPPED?   ☐ SENT/GIVEN?

NOTES

NAME

GIFT IDEAS

BUDGET   ACTUAL

STORE/GIFT

☐ ORDERED?   ☐ WRAPPED?   ☐ SENT/GIVEN?

NOTES

NAME

GIFT IDEAS

BUDGET   ACTUAL

STORE/GIFT

☐ ORDERED?   ☐ WRAPPED?   ☐ SENT/GIVEN?

NOTES

NAME

GIFT IDEAS

BUDGET   ACTUAL

STORE/GIFT

☐ ORDERED?   ☐ WRAPPED? ☐ SENT/GIVEN?

NOTES

NAME

GIFT IDEAS

BUDGET   ACTUAL

STORE/GIFT

☐ ORDERED?   ☐ WRAPPED? ☐ SENT/GIVEN?

NOTES

NAME

GIFT IDEAS

BUDGET   ACTUAL

STORE/GIFT

☐ ORDERED?   ☐ WRAPPED?   ☐ SENT/GIVEN?

NOTES

NAME

GIFT IDEAS

BUDGET   ACTUAL

STORE/GIFT

☐ ORDERED?   ☐ WRAPPED?   ☐ SENT/GIVEN?

NOTES

NAME

GIFT IDEAS

BUDGET   ACTUAL

STORE/GIFT

☐ ORDERED?   ☐ WRAPPED?   ☐ SENT/GIVEN?

NOTES

NAME

GIFT IDEAS

BUDGET   ACTUAL

STORE/GIFT

☐ ORDERED?   ☐ WRAPPED? ☐ SENT/GIVEN?

NOTES

NAME

GIFT IDEAS

BUDGET ACTUAL

STORE/GIFT

☐ ORDERED? ☐ WRAPPED? ☐ SENT/GIVEN?

NOTES

NAME

GIFT IDEAS

BUDGET   ACTUAL

STORE/GIFT

☐ ORDERED?   ☐ WRAPPED?   ☐ SENT/GIVEN?

NOTES

NAME

GIFT IDEAS

BUDGET   ACTUAL

STORE/GIFT

☐ ORDERED?   ☐ WRAPPED?   ☐ SENT/GIVEN?

NOTES

NAME

GIFT IDEAS

BUDGET   ACTUAL

STORE/GIFT

☐ ORDERED?   ☐ WRAPPED? ☐ SENT/GIVEN?

NOTES

NAME

GIFT IDEAS

BUDGET   ACTUAL

STORE/GIFT

☐ ORDERED?   ☐ WRAPPED?   ☐ SENT/GIVEN?

NOTES

NAME

GIFT IDEAS

BUDGET   ACTUAL

STORE/GIFT

☐ ORDERED?   ☐ WRAPPED? ☐ SENT/GIVEN?

NOTES

NAME

GIFT IDEAS

BUDGET   ACTUAL

STORE/GIFT

☐ ORDERED?   ☐ WRAPPED?   ☐ SENT/GIVEN?

NOTES

NAME

GIFT IDEAS

BUDGET   ACTUAL

STORE/GIFT

☐ ORDERED?   ☐ WRAPPED? ☐ SENT/GIVEN?

NOTES

NAME

GIFT IDEAS

BUDGET   ACTUAL

STORE/GIFT

☐ ORDERED?   ☐ WRAPPED?   ☐ SENT/GIVEN?

NOTES

NAME

GIFT IDEAS

BUDGET   ACTUAL

STORE/GIFT

☐ ORDERED?   ☐ WRAPPED?   ☐ SENT/GIVEN?

NOTES

NAME

GIFT IDEAS

BUDGET   ACTUAL

STORE/GIFT

☐ ORDERED?   ☐ WRAPPED?   ☐ SENT/GIVEN?

NOTES

NAME

GIFT IDEAS

BUDGET   ACTUAL

STORE/GIFT

☐ ORDERED?   ☐ WRAPPED? ☐ SENT/GIVEN?

NOTES

NAME

GIFT IDEAS

BUDGET   ACTUAL

STORE/GIFT

☐ ORDERED?   ☐ WRAPPED? ☐ SENT/GIVEN?

NOTES

NAME

GIFT IDEAS

BUDGET   ACTUAL

STORE/GIFT

☐ ORDERED?   ☐ WRAPPED? ☐ SENT/GIVEN?

NOTES

NAME

GIFT IDEAS

BUDGET   ACTUAL

STORE/GIFT

☐ ORDERED?   ☐ WRAPPED?   ☐ SENT/GIVEN?

NOTES

NAME

GIFT IDEAS

BUDGET   ACTUAL

STORE/GIFT

☐ ORDERED?   ☐ WRAPPED? ☐ SENT/GIVEN?

NOTES

NAME

GIFT IDEAS

BUDGET   ACTUAL

STORE/GIFT

☐ ORDERED?   ☐ WRAPPED?   ☐ SENT/GIVEN?

NOTES

NAME

GIFT IDEAS

BUDGET   ACTUAL

STORE/GIFT

☐ ORDERED?   ☐ WRAPPED? ☐ SENT/GIVEN?

NOTES

NAME

GIFT IDEAS

BUDGET   ACTUAL

STORE/GIFT

☐ ORDERED?   ☐ WRAPPED? ☐ SENT/GIVEN?

NOTES

NAME

GIFT IDEAS

BUDGET   ACTUAL

STORE/GIFT

☐ ORDERED?   ☐ WRAPPED? ☐ SENT/GIVEN?

NOTES

NAME

GIFT IDEAS

BUDGET   ACTUAL

STORE/GIFT

☐ ORDERED?   ☐ WRAPPED? ☐ SENT/GIVEN?

NOTES

NAME

GIFT IDEAS

BUDGET   ACTUAL

STORE/GIFT

☐ ORDERED?   ☐ WRAPPED? ☐ SENT/GIVEN?

NOTES

NAME

GIFT IDEAS

BUDGET   ACTUAL

STORE/GIFT

☐ ORDERED?   ☐ WRAPPED? ☐ SENT/GIVEN?

NOTES

NAME

GIFT IDEAS

BUDGET   ACTUAL

STORE/GIFT

☐ ORDERED?   ☐ WRAPPED? ☐ SENT/GIVEN?

NOTES

NAME

GIFT IDEAS

BUDGET   ACTUAL

STORE/GIFT

☐ ORDERED?   ☐ WRAPPED?   ☐ SENT/GIVEN?

NOTES

NAME

GIFT IDEAS

BUDGET   ACTUAL

STORE/GIFT

☐ ORDERED?   ☐ WRAPPED? ☐ SENT/GIVEN?

NOTES

NAME

GIFT IDEAS

BUDGET   ACTUAL

STORE/GIFT

☐ ORDERED?   ☐ WRAPPED?   ☐ SENT/GIVEN?

NOTES

NAME

GIFT IDEAS

BUDGET   ACTUAL

STORE/GIFT

☐ ORDERED?   ☐ WRAPPED?   ☐ SENT/GIVEN?

NOTES

NAME

GIFT IDEAS

BUDGET   ACTUAL

STORE/GIFT

☐ ORDERED?   ☐ WRAPPED?   ☐ SENT/GIVEN?

NOTES

NAME

GIFT IDEAS

BUDGET   ACTUAL

STORE/GIFT

☐ ORDERED?   ☐ WRAPPED?   ☐ SENT/GIVEN?

NOTES

NAME

GIFT IDEAS

BUDGET   ACTUAL

STORE/GIFT

☐ ORDERED?   ☐ WRAPPED? ☐ SENT/GIVEN?

NOTES

NAME

GIFT IDEAS

BUDGET   ACTUAL

STORE/GIFT

☐ ORDERED?   ☐ WRAPPED?   ☐ SENT/GIVEN?

NOTES

NAME

GIFT IDEAS

BUDGET   ACTUAL

STORE/GIFT

☐ ORDERED?   ☐ WRAPPED?   ☐ SENT/GIVEN?

NOTES

Made in the USA
Coppell, TX
24 March 2022

75446582R00057